MEL BAY PRESENTS

# Flamenco Music for Acoustic Guitar

## BY MEL AGEN

Much has been said about flamenco guitar and the techniques used in this style of playing. Two words are essential in understanding and acquiring a feeling for this music. The words are *technique* and *falseta* and they mean the same thing.

In flamenco think of the name of the piece of music as being the entire melody. Now think of each falseta as being a melody within a melody. Each falseta usually begins and ends with a particular technique, so each time you see a different finger pattern emerge you can be quite sure you have come to a new falseta. It is the synthesis of the various falsetas or techniques in a piece that lends the character and mood to the composition. All the parts add up to create the total feeling of any song.

## CD CONTENTS

# EDITOR'S NOTE

MEL AGEN

Flamenco music has a style and character all its own. It is bristling with life. We feel that the arrangements contained in this book embody the very essence of that fiery and moody style. Mel Agen has spent many years studying and performing Flamenco music. His mastery of the subject emerges throughout the many arrangements contained in this text.

Wm. Bay

Author's Note:

Traditionally, students of flamenco guitar learned the art in the time-honored aural fashion. The fire and varied moods of flamenco music are the natural result of this aural tradition, its improvised nature, and its original function as dance accompaniment. Some of these moods cannot be communicated effectively in standard notation or tablature, and it is common knowledge that in written flamenco guitar music all passages are open to individual interpretation.

In flamenco parlance, such passages are referred to as *falsetas*. These measures or phrases can be played *ad libitum*, literally "as one pleases"—or they may be varied or even omitted according to the whim or ability of the guitarist. Try this approach with the *Farruca* or *Petemeras*, or any flamenco piece. From these expansions, compressions, and dynamic variations come the very life and essence of flamenco music as well as the unique styles of such artists as Serrano, Sabicas, Montoya, Escudero, and others.

# CONTENTS

# THE CORRECT WAY TO HOLD THE GUITAR

### (TWO WAYS SHOWN)

1. The Left Leg Crossed over the Right.

2. Placing the Left Foot on a Small Stool.

## THE RIGHT HAND
## (R. H.)

### THE RIGHT HAND FINGERS WILL BE DESIGNATED AS

1 = I

2 = M

3 = A

Thumb = P

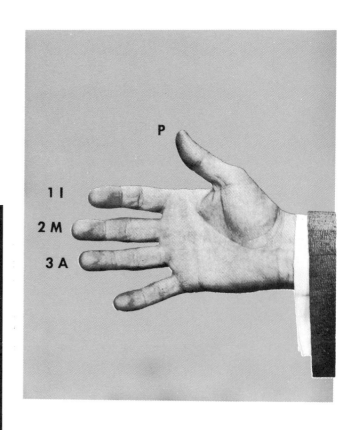

### THE NAMES OF THE R. H. FINGERS ARE:

| (English) | (ABV) | (Spanish) |
|-----------|-------|-----------|
| 1st — Index | (I) | Indice |
| 2nd — Middle | (M) | Medio |
| 3rd — Ring | (A) | Anular |
| Thumb — | (P) | Pulgar |

4

# FLAMENCO GUITAR TECHNIQUES

**Rasgueado** — Strumming chords in a very percussive manner by using Down and Up Strokes of the various fingers.

GENERAL
MOTION

(largest strings to smallest)

(smallest strings to largest)

SPECIFIC
SYMBOLS

Downstroke (largest to smallest strings) using first the anular, then middle, then index fingers in rapid sequence.

Downstroke (largest to smallest strings) using only the index finger.

Upstroke (smallest toargest strings) using only the index finger.

This Symbol is found in the piece Bulerias. It means to tap the top of the guitar with the anular (3rd or ring) finger. At the same time, bring the index finger down across the strings. ( ↑ )

**Picado** — Plucking the strings alternately with the index, middle or ring fingers of the right hand.

# HOW TO READ TABLATURE

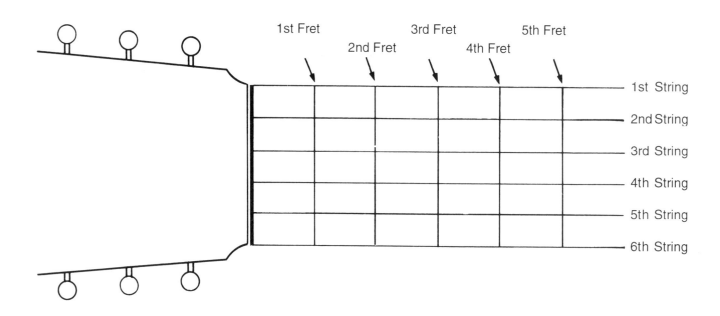

In tablature the lines represent strings. The numbers appearing on the lines indicate frets. (O = open string). In the following example a C chord would be played. (1st string open, 2nd string press down on the 1st fret, 3rd string open, 4th string press down on the 2nd fret, 5th string press down on the 3rd fret, and finally do not play the 6th string.

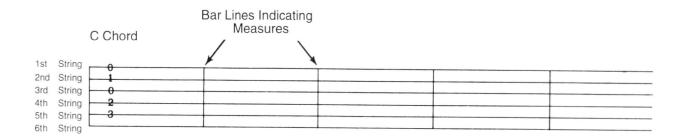

# PETENERAS DE ESPAÑA

M. Agen

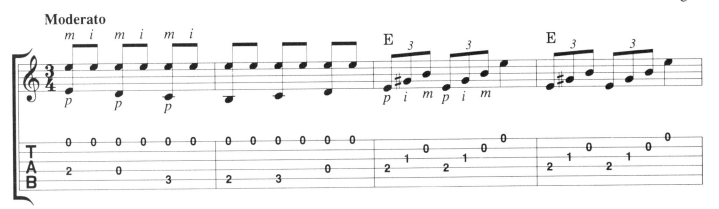

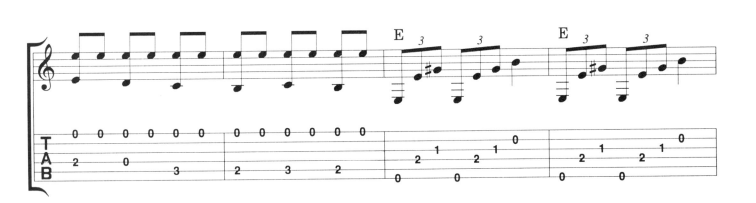

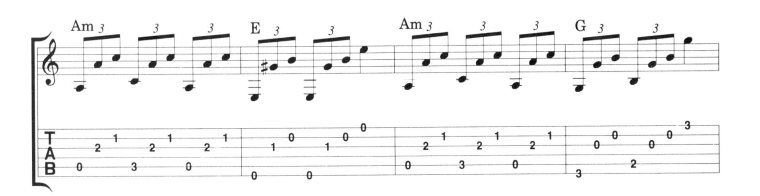

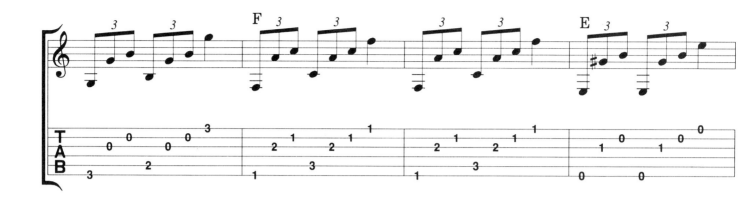

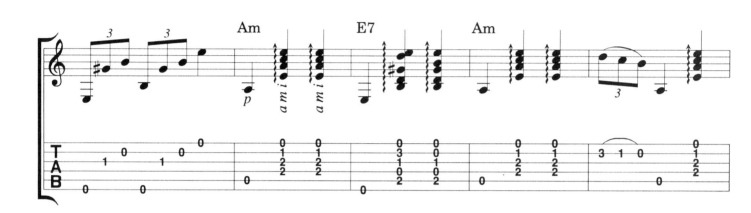

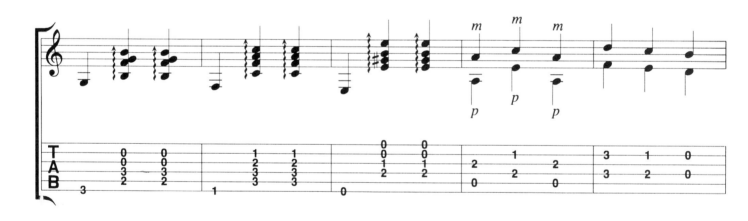

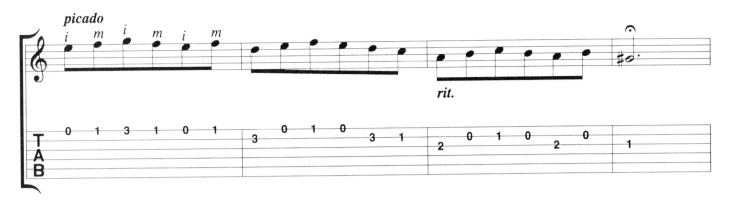

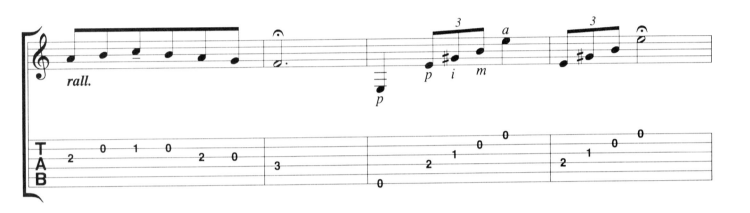

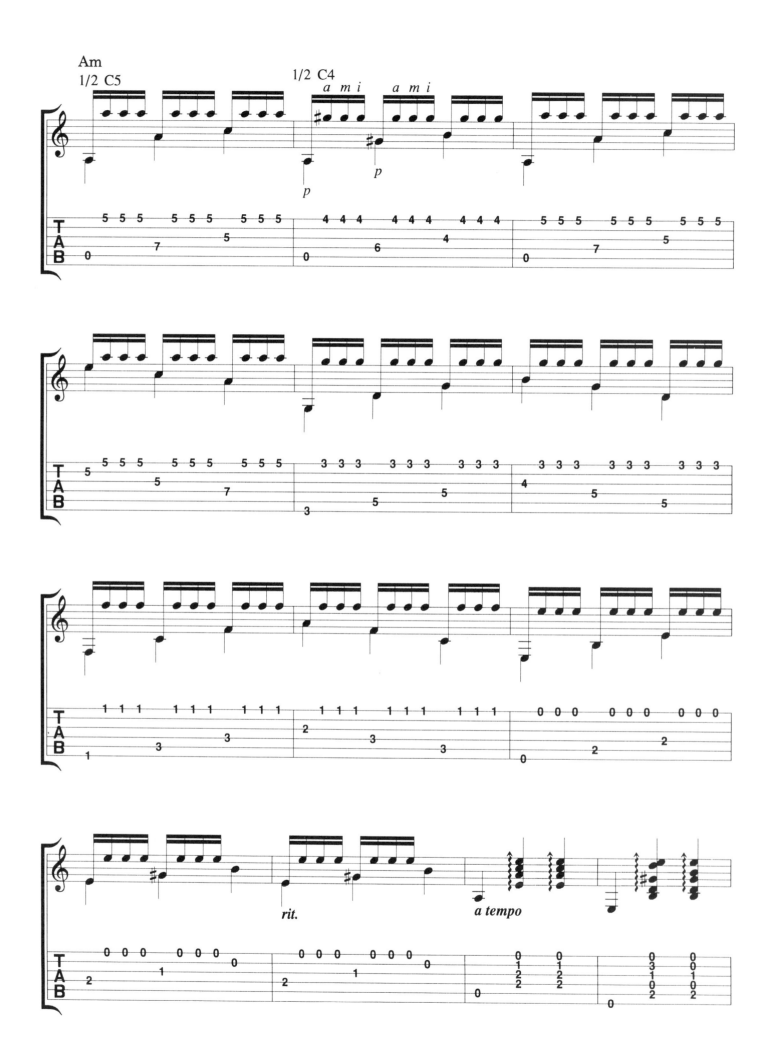

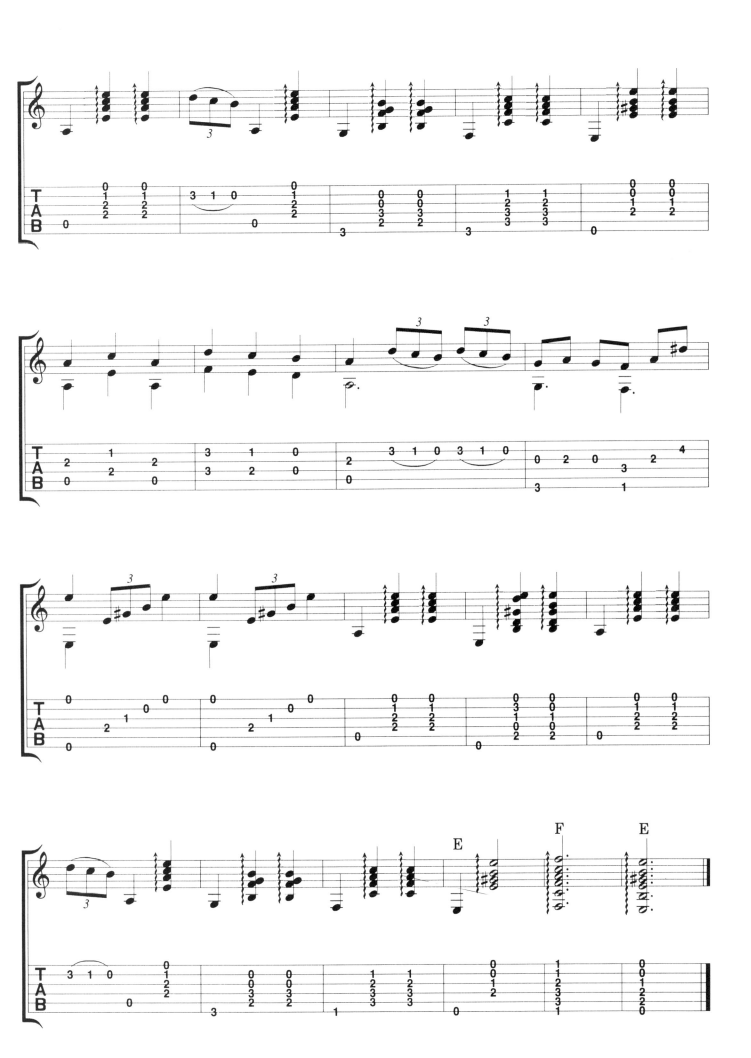

# SOLEARES
### (De Montes)

M. Agen

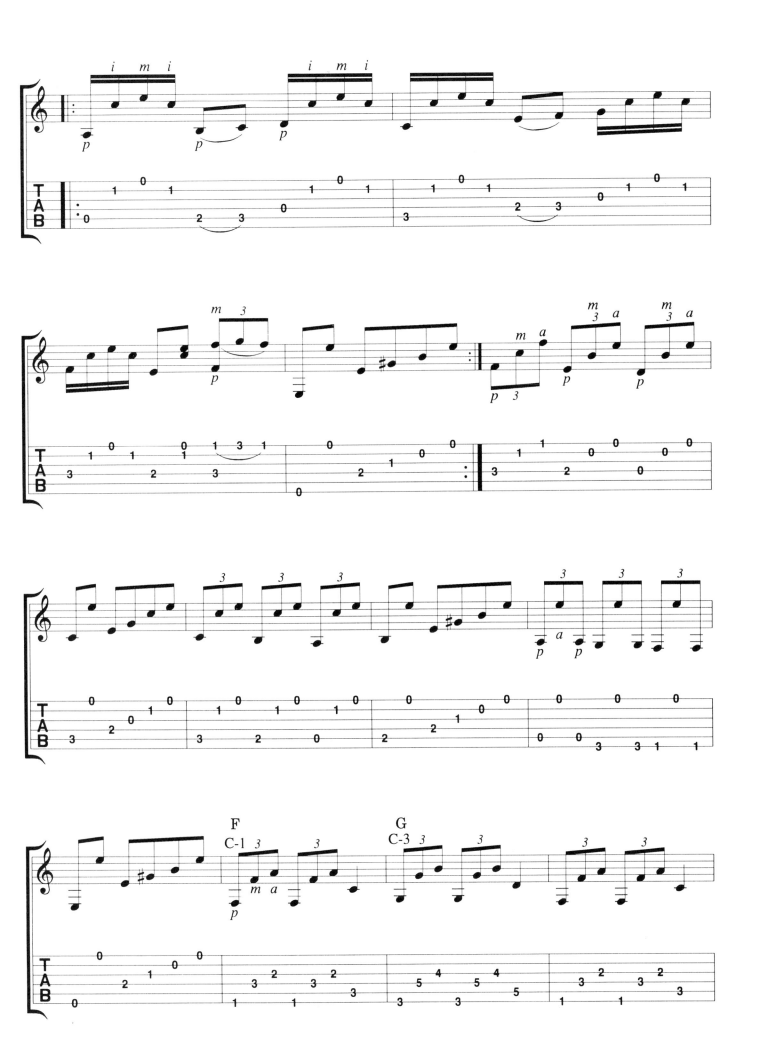

13

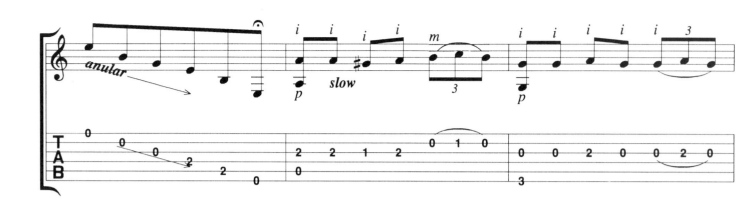

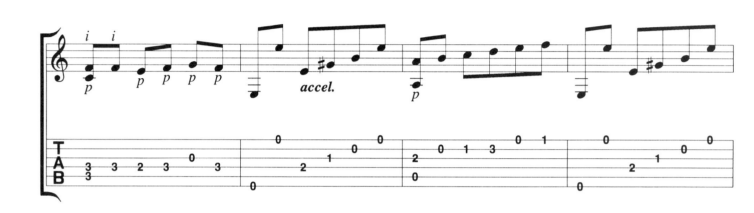

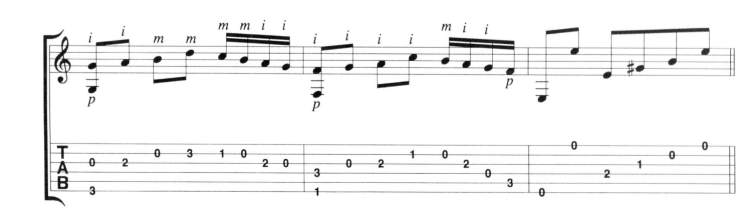

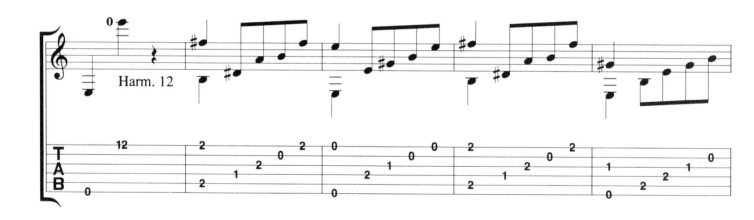

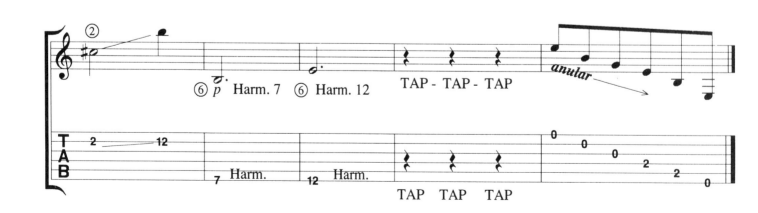

# FARRUCA DE JUERGA

M. Agen

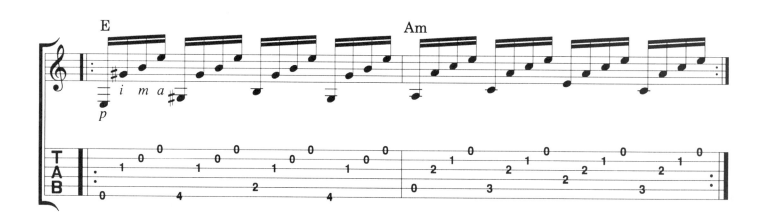

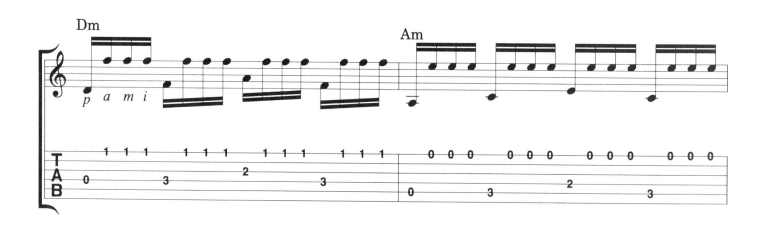

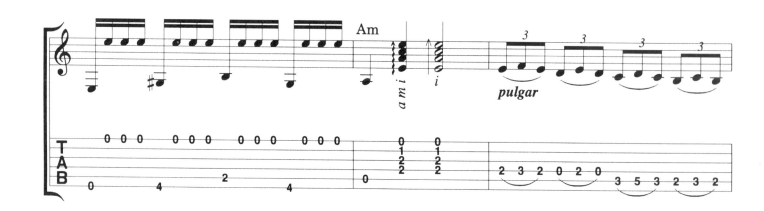

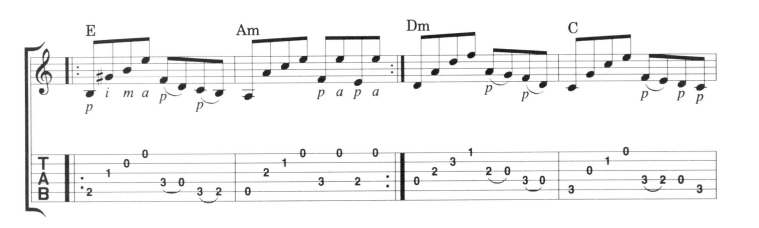

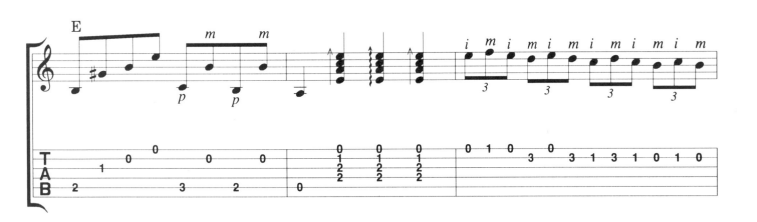

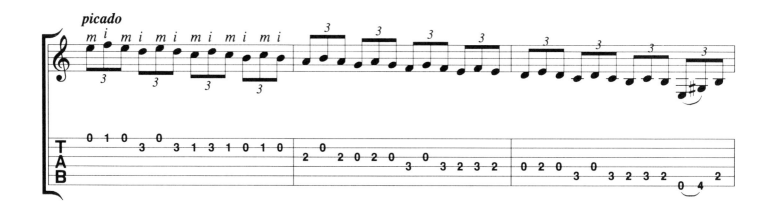

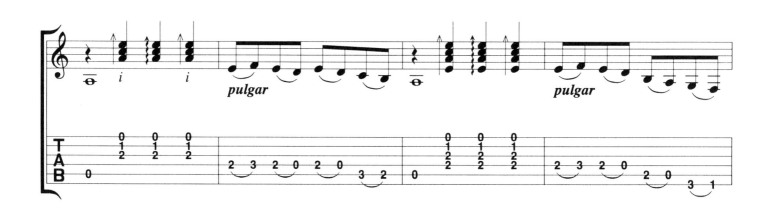

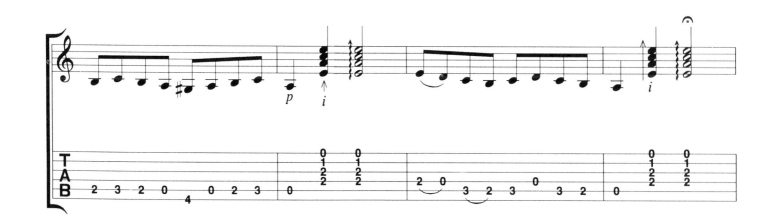

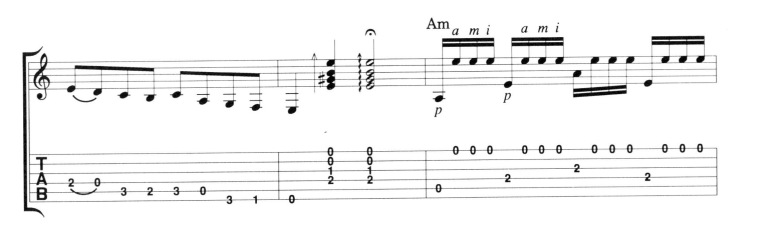
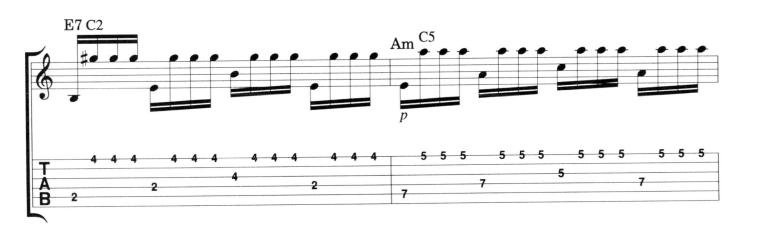
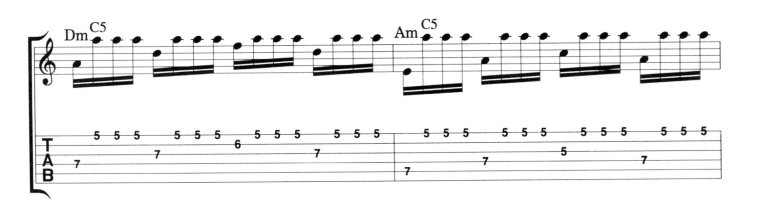
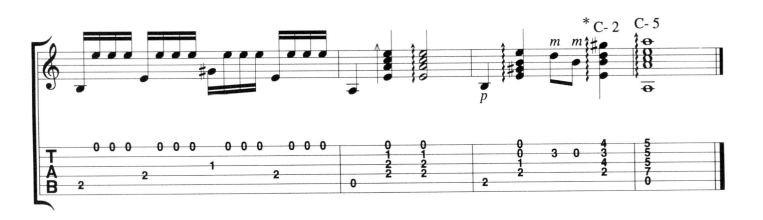

# CARACOLES

M. Agen

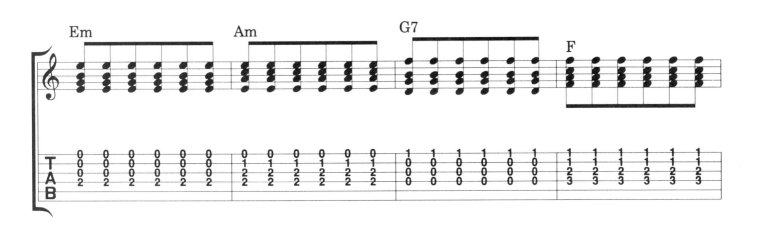

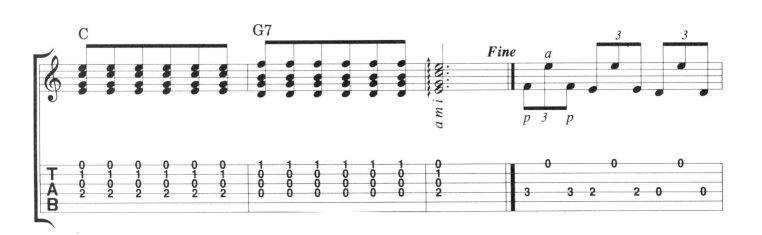

23

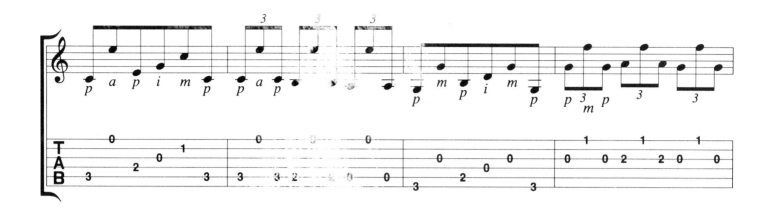

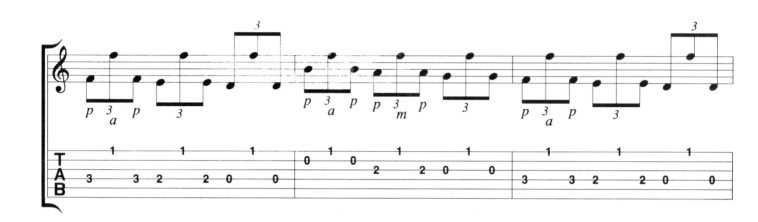

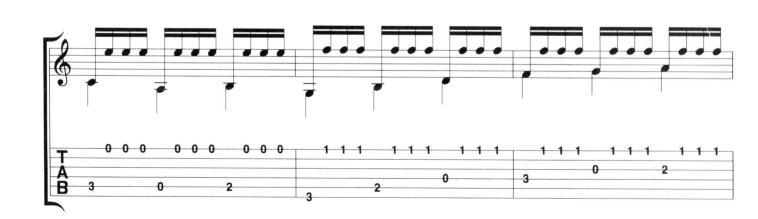

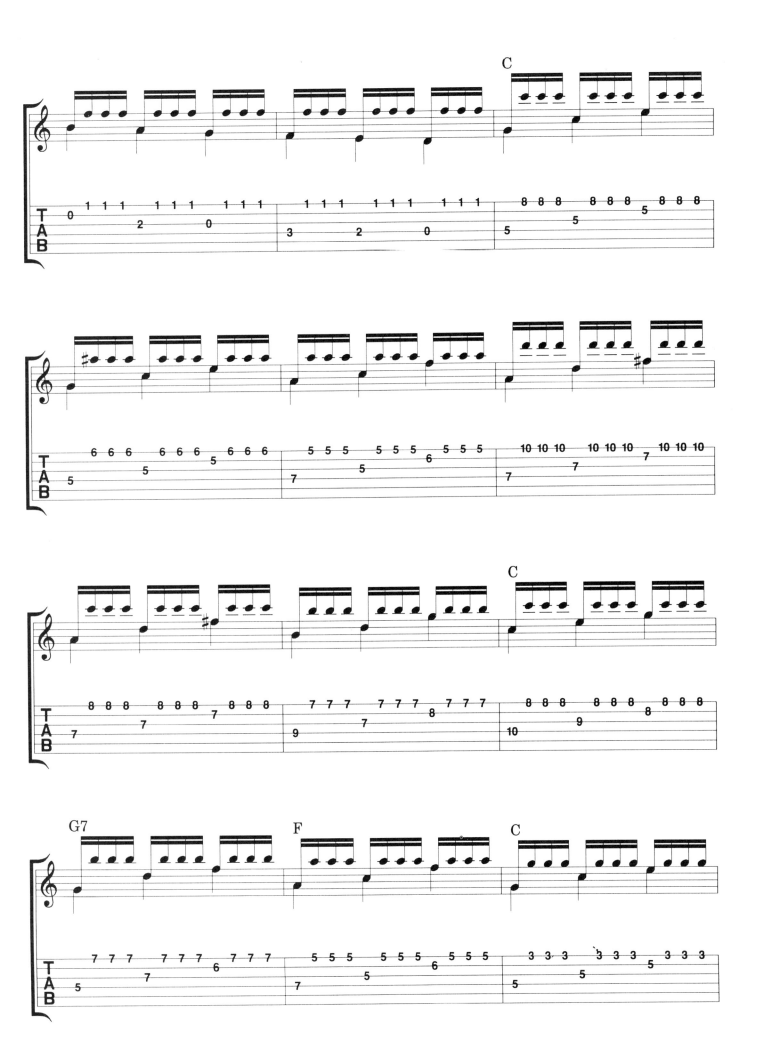

25

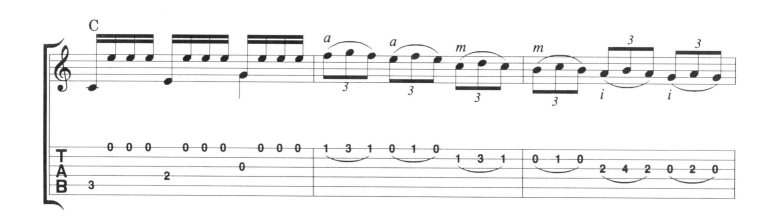

# MALAGUEÑA DEL SOÑADOR

M.Agen

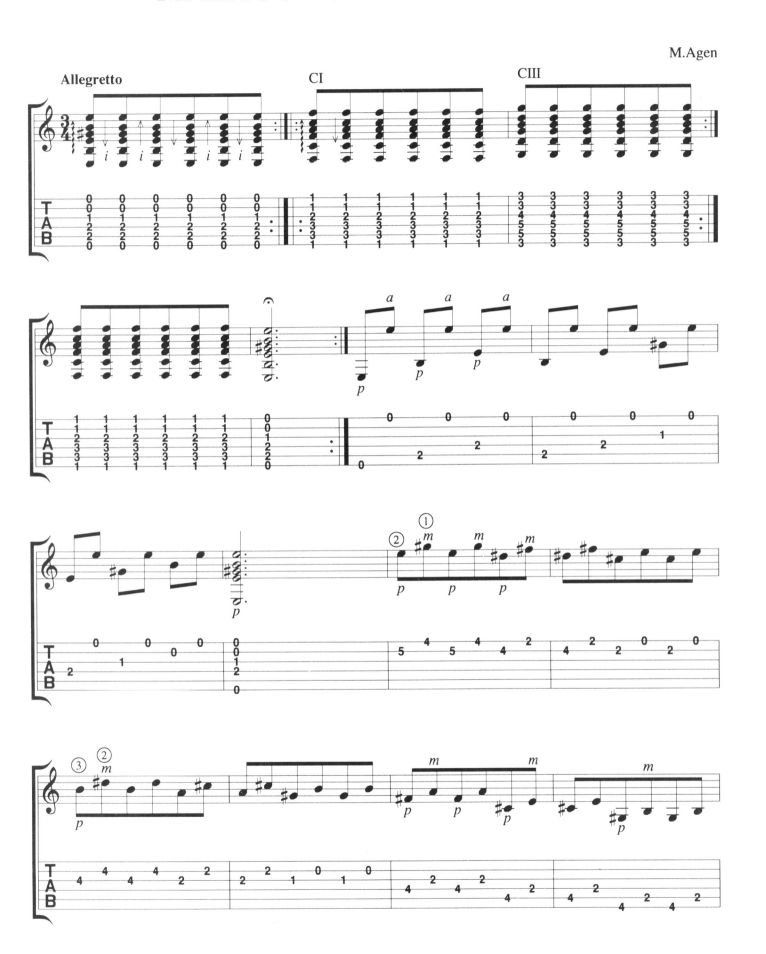

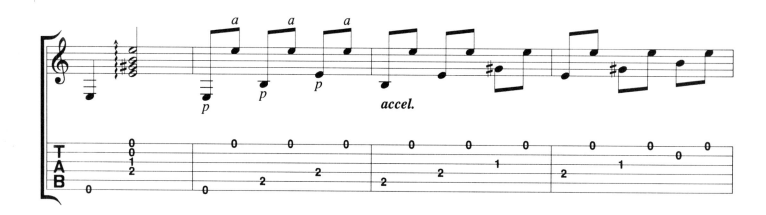

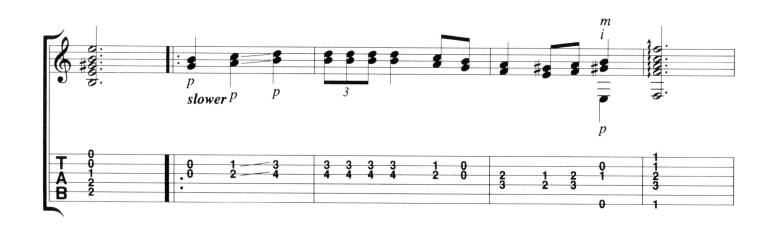

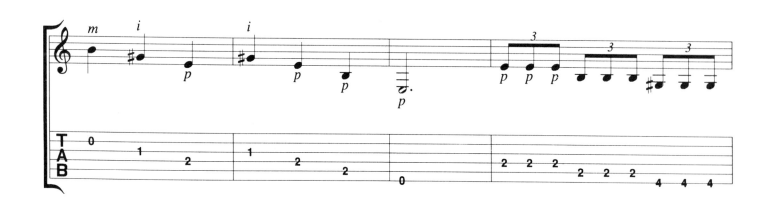

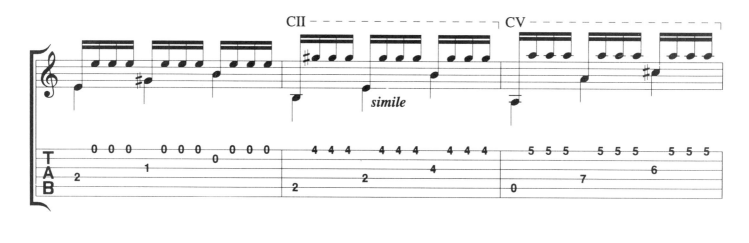

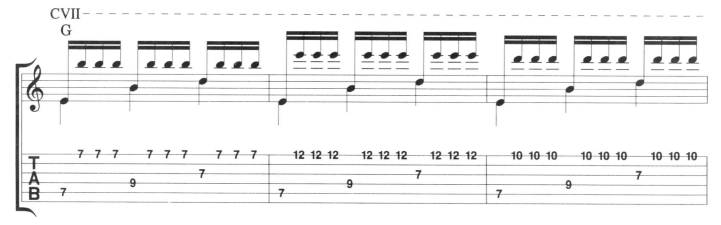

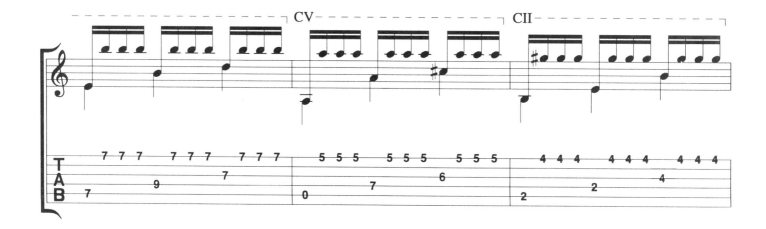

G chord full bar on 7th fret lasts four measures, only small finger moves to get higher notes.

# BULERIAS

M Agen

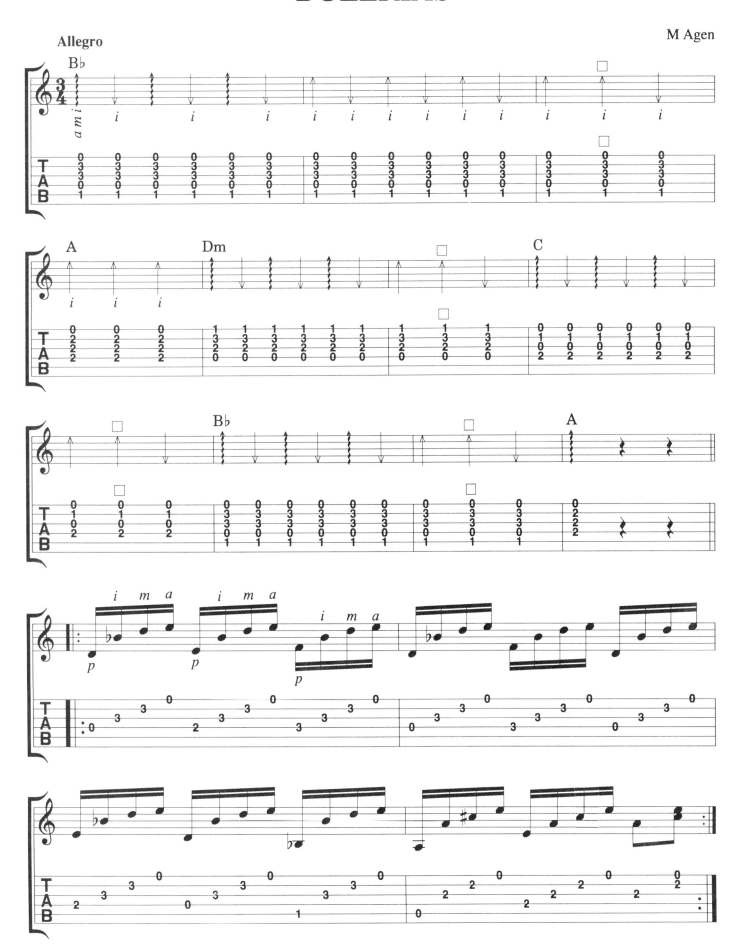

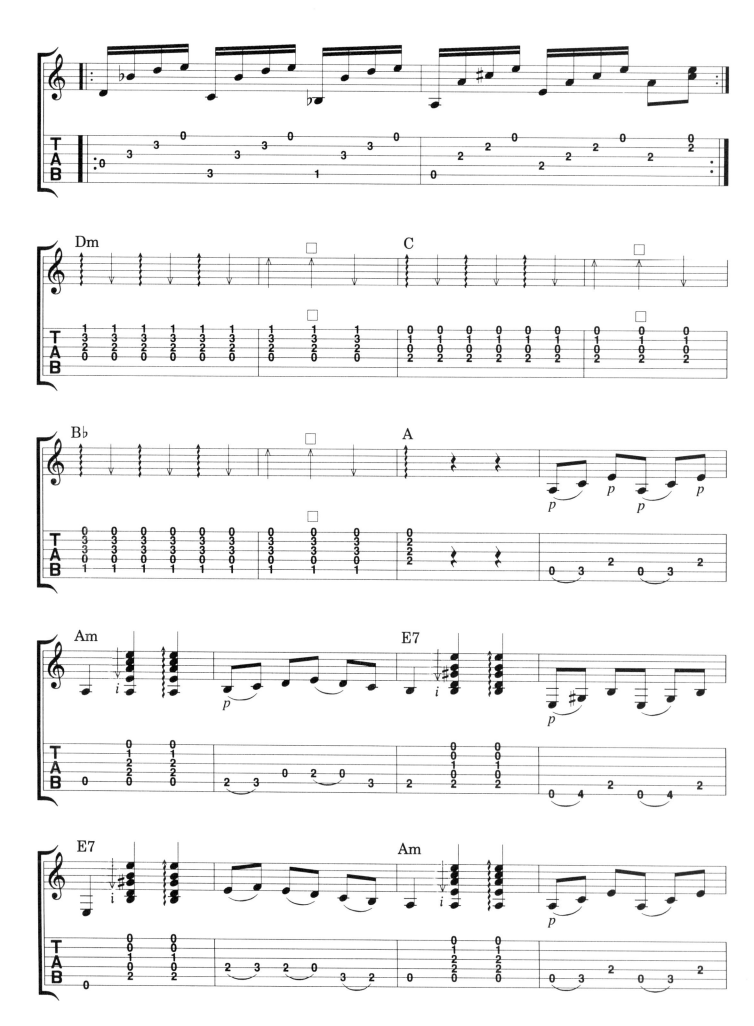

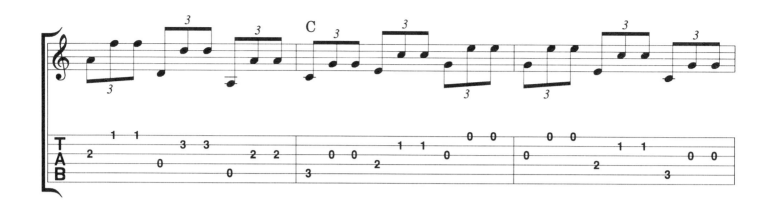

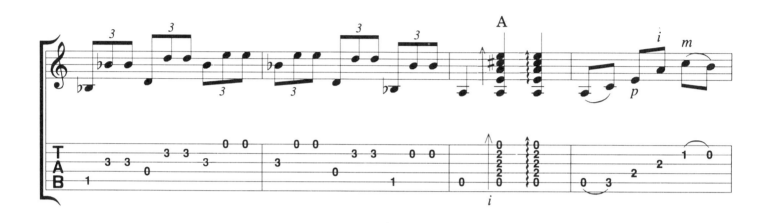

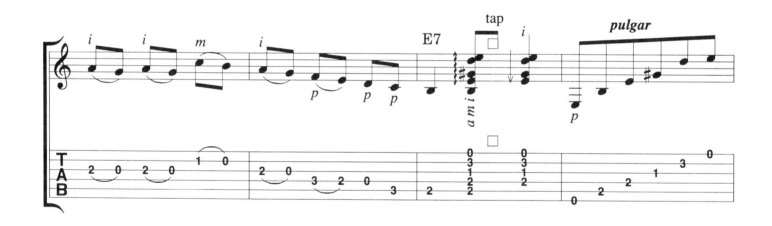

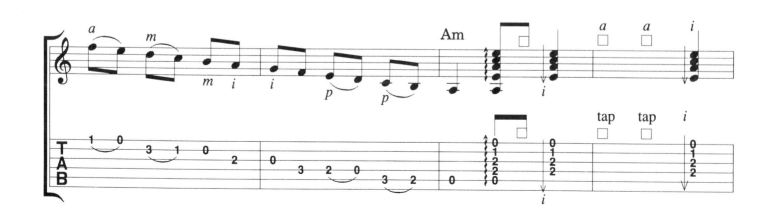

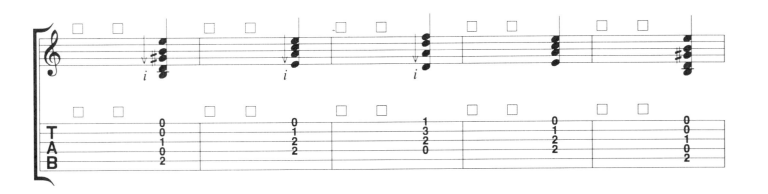

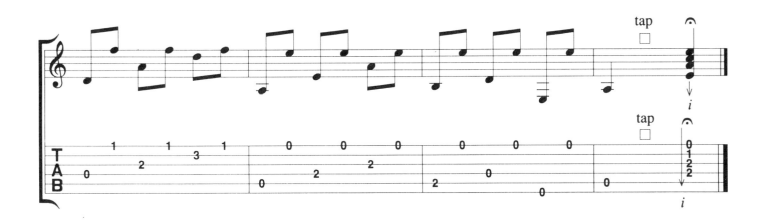

# SEGUIRIYAS

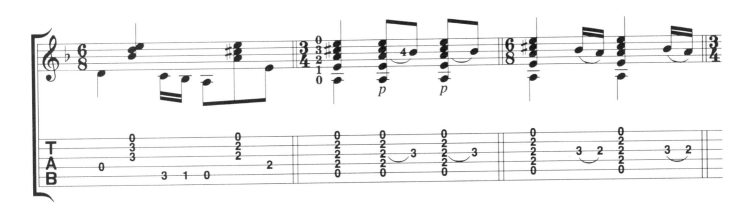

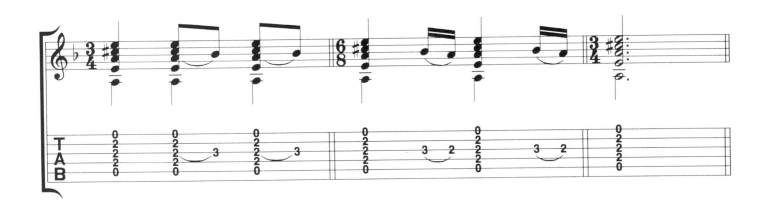

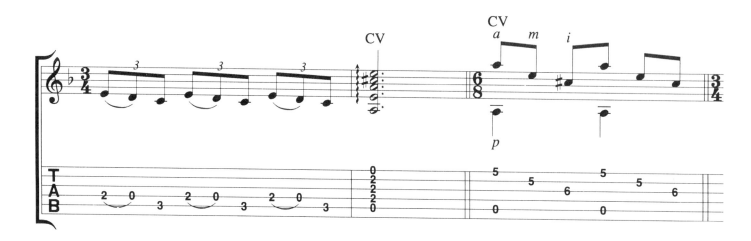

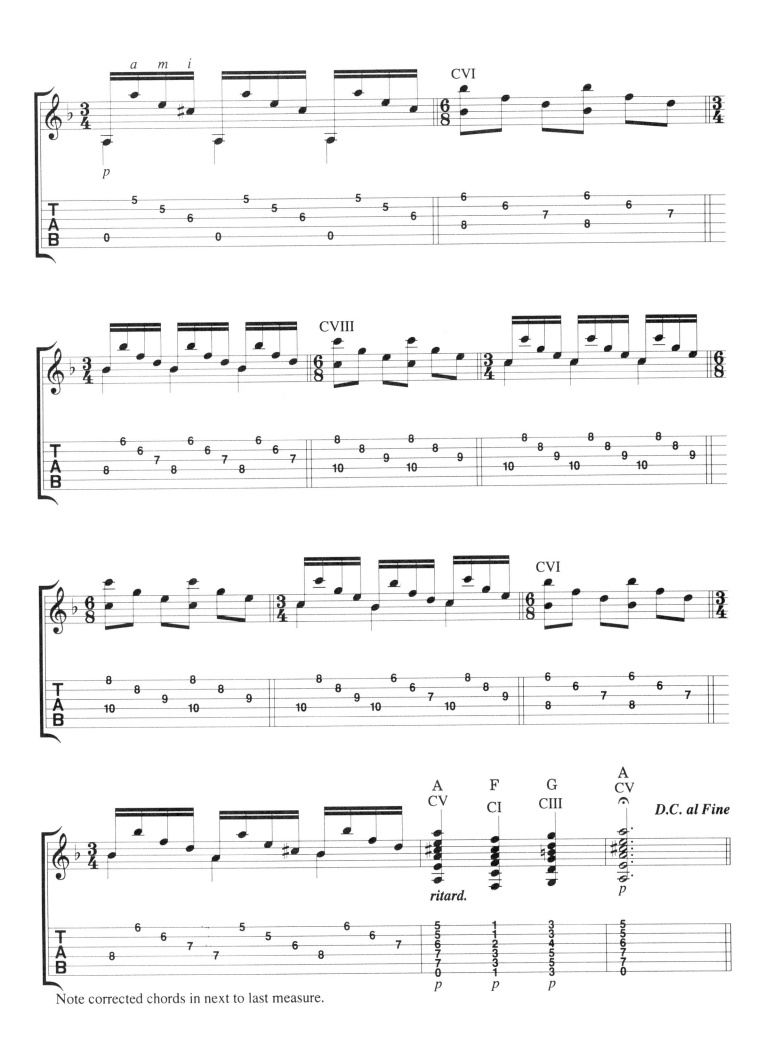

Note corrected chords in next to last measure.

# MALAGA CITY OF DREAMS

## (Tremolo Study)

By Mel Agen

**With Feeling**
**Andante**

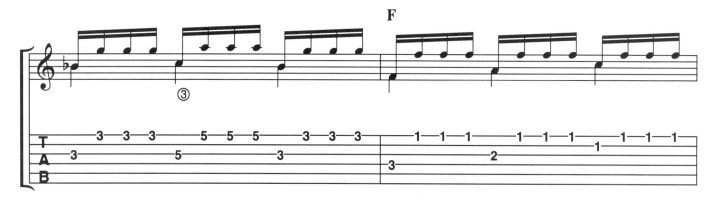

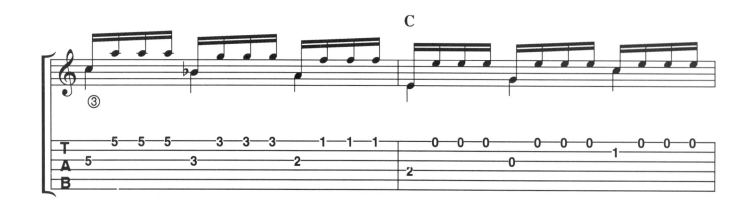

C

CIII
G

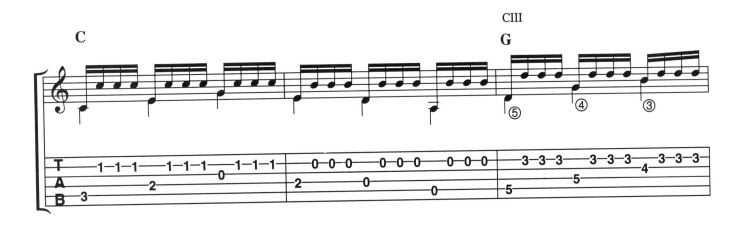

F

E

41

**F**

**Em**          **Am**          **Dm**

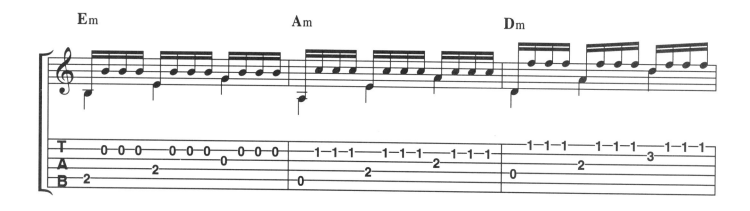

*D.C.*

*Repeat entire piece 1x*

Advanced artists repeat one octave higher then return to base.

# AMANTE
## (Peteneras)

**Moderato**

By Mel Agen

CIII

CI

*Fine*

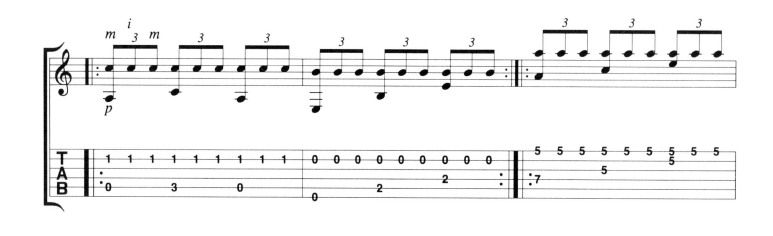
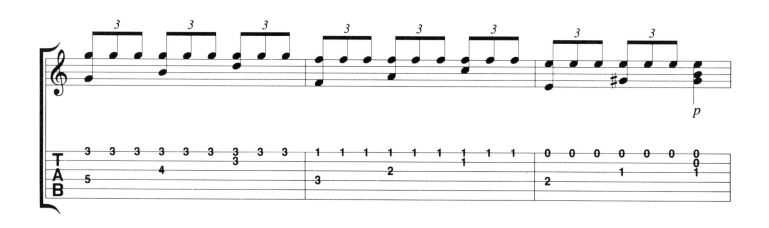
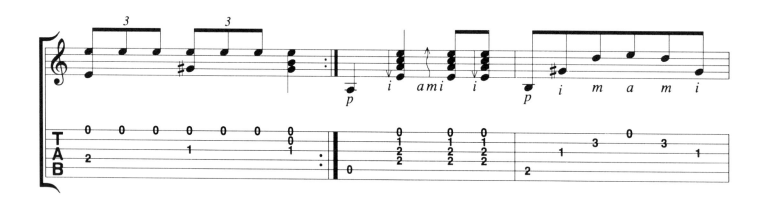
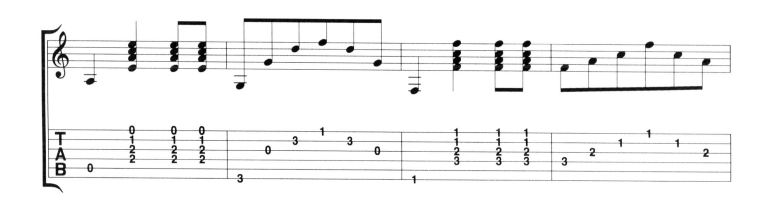

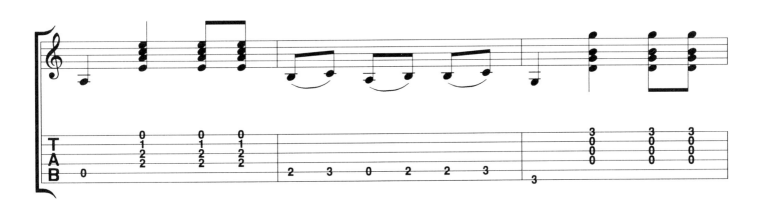

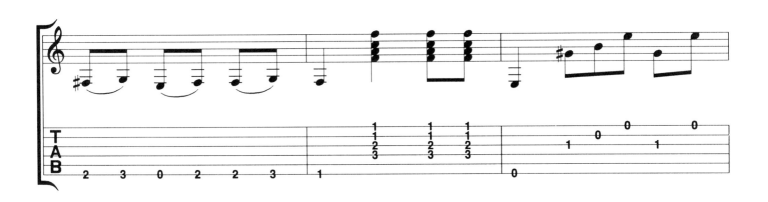

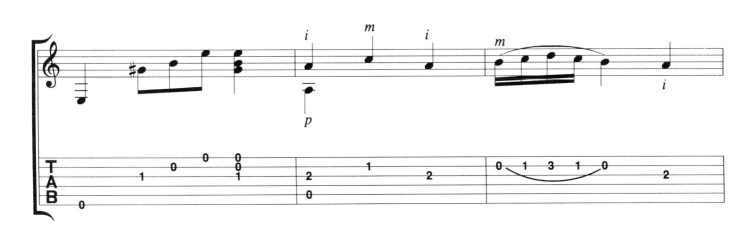

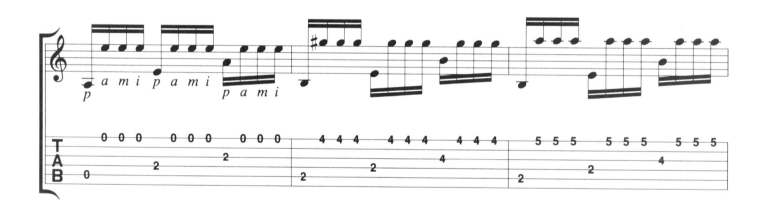

# SANGRE DE GITANO

Guitar Solo
by Mel Agen

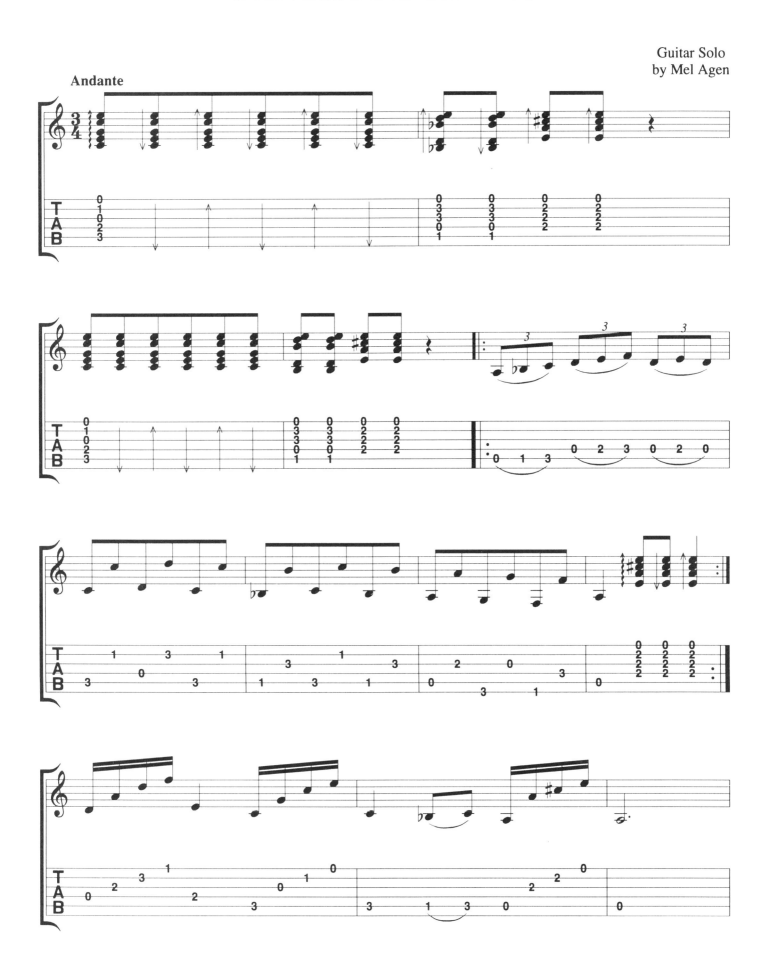

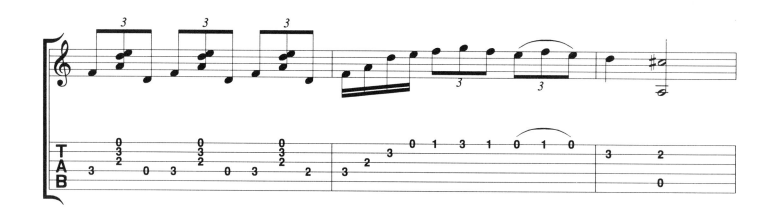
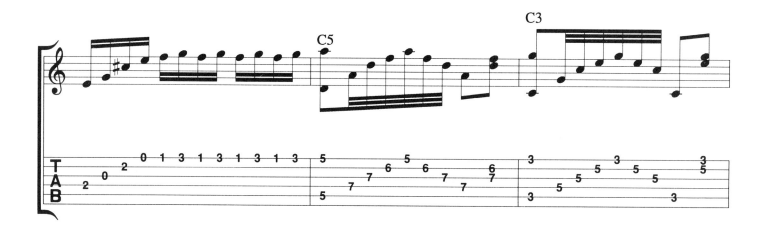

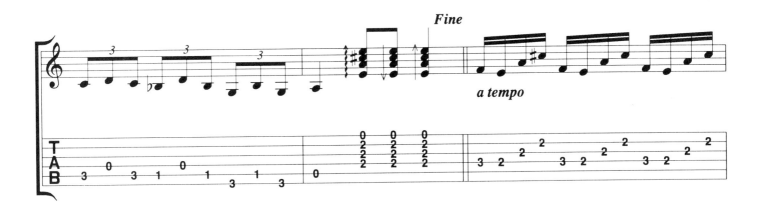

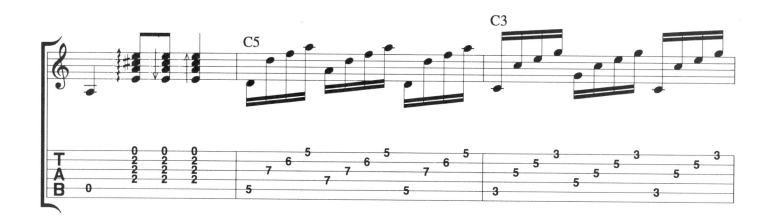

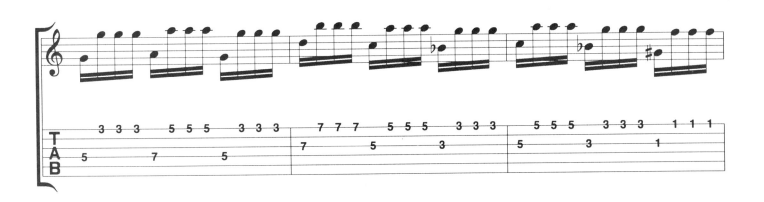

# ANHELO
## (Old Time Soleares)

By Mel Agen

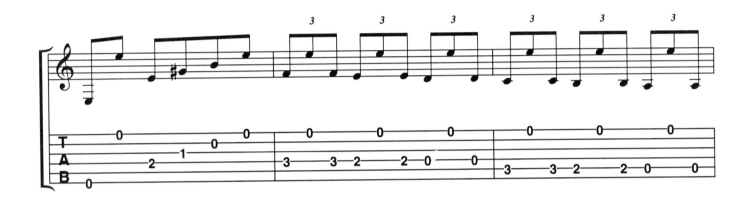

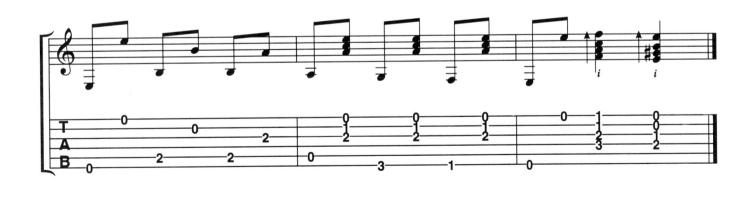

# CANELA

By Mel Agen

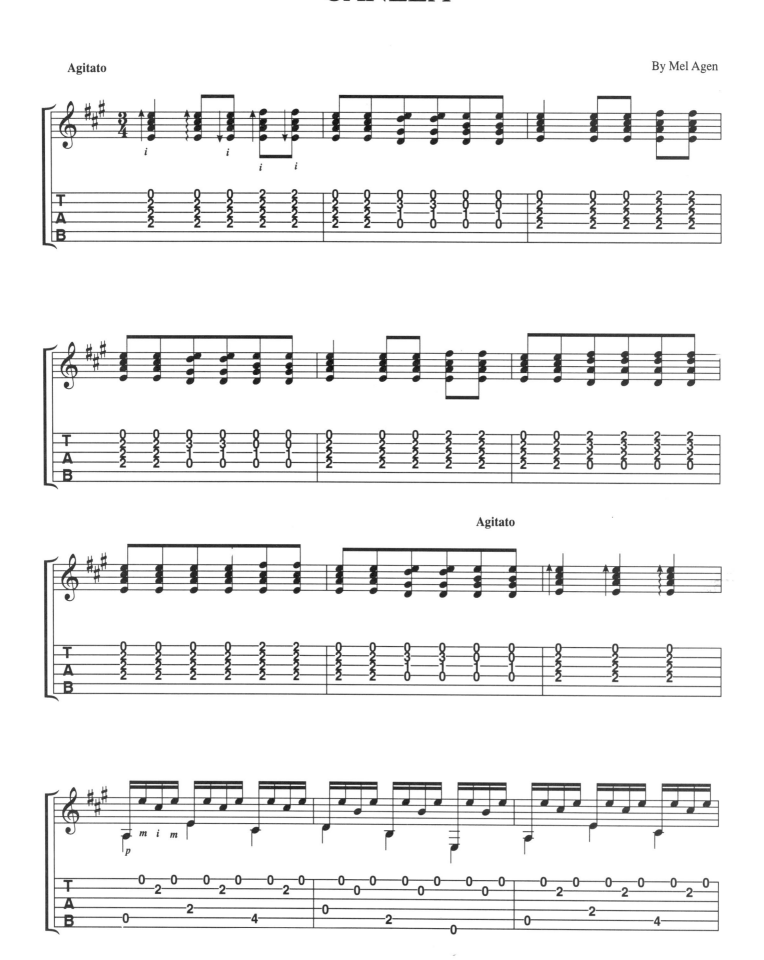

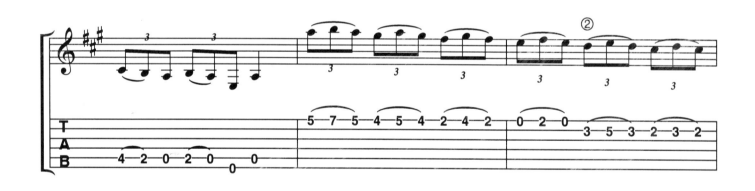

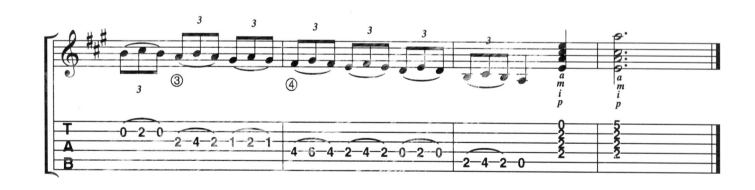

# GRANADINAS

M. Agen

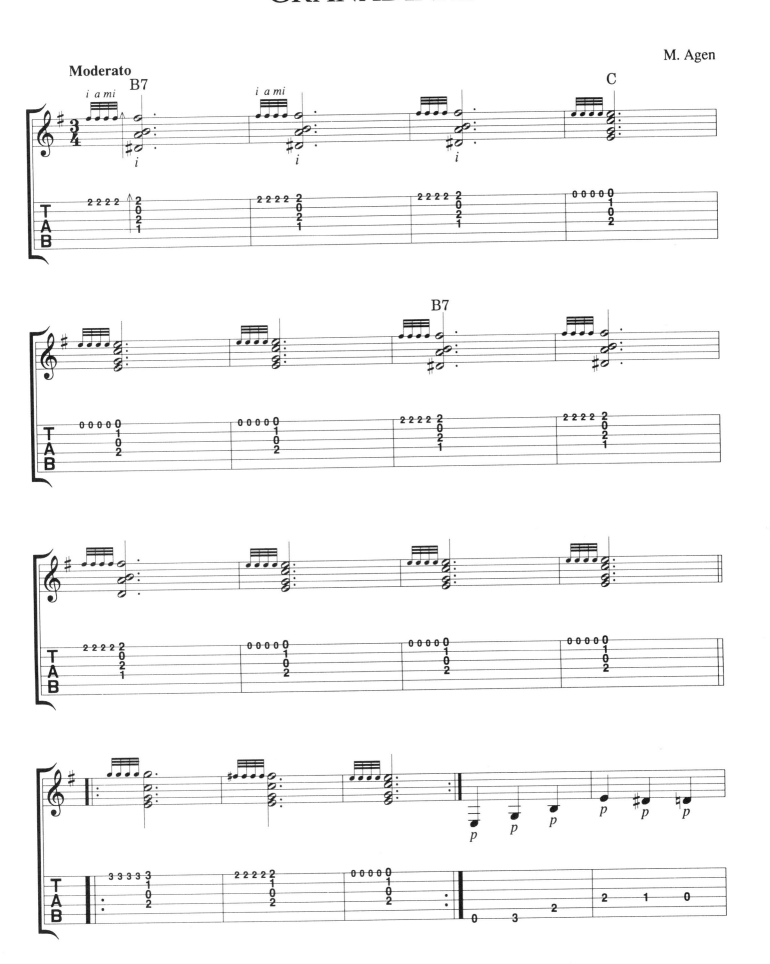

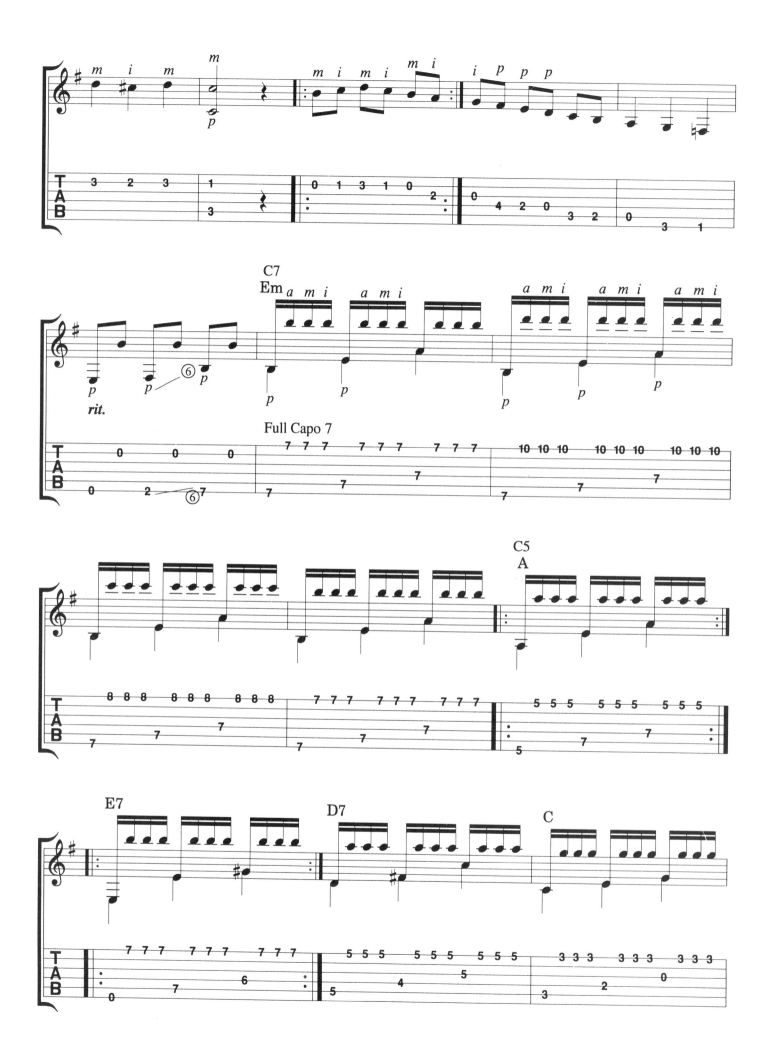

58

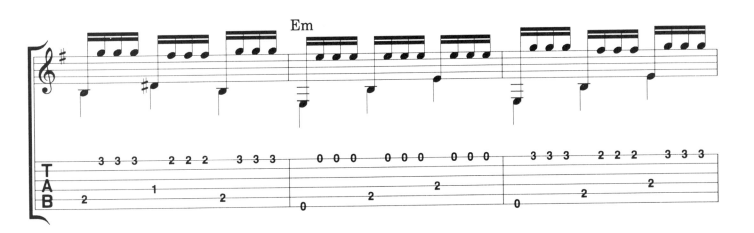

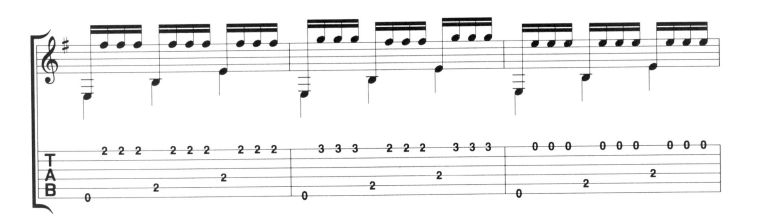

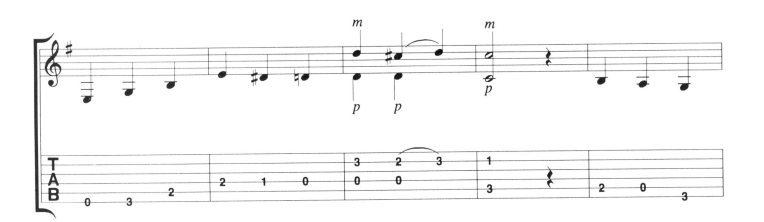

# GUAJIRAS

M. Agen

*pulgar to end of falseta*

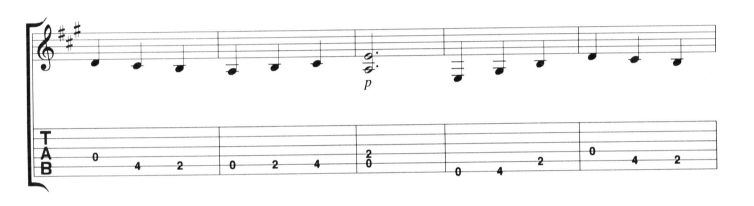

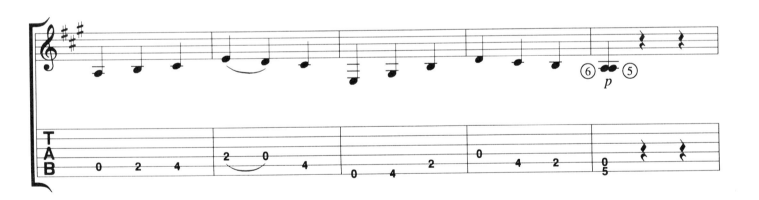

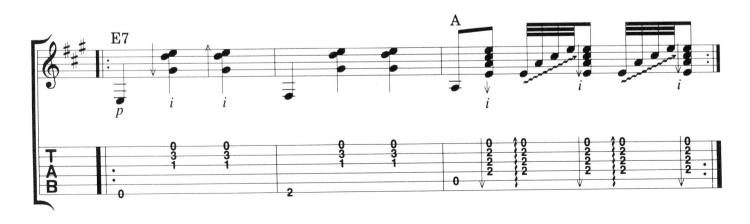

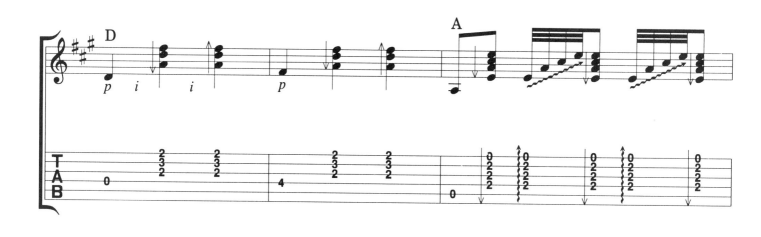

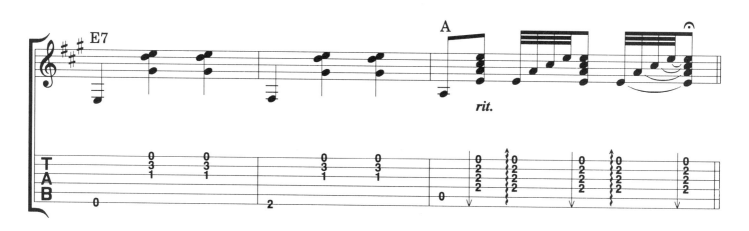

63

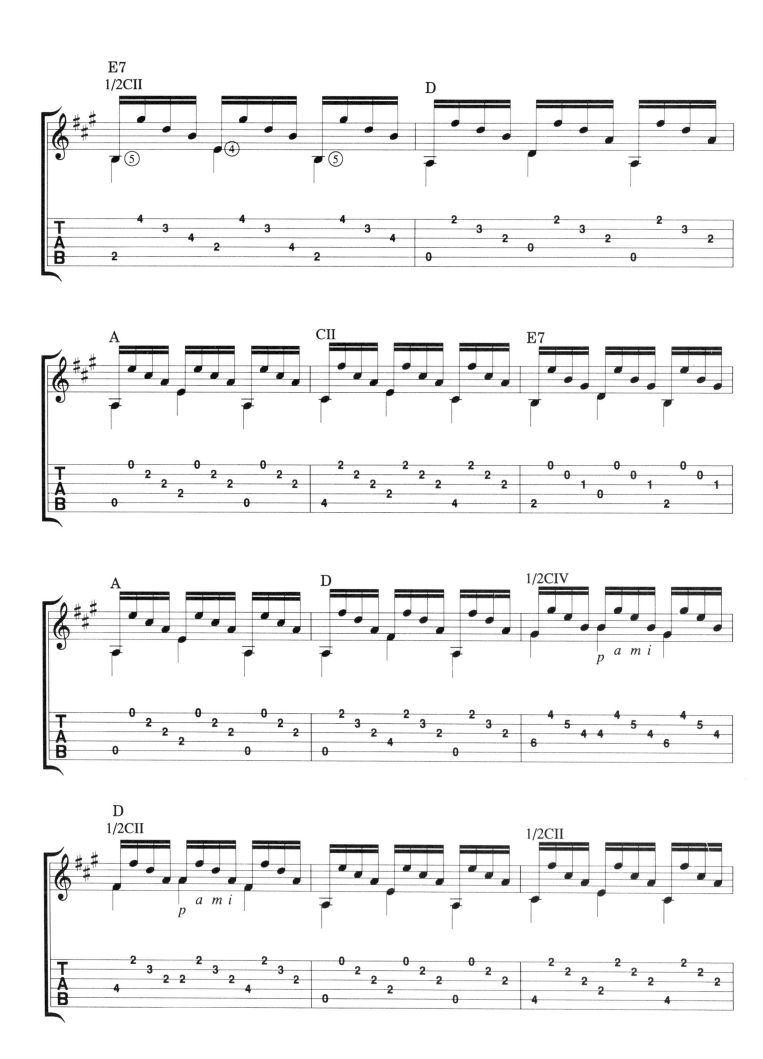

# ALEGRIAS DE MOFA

M. Agen

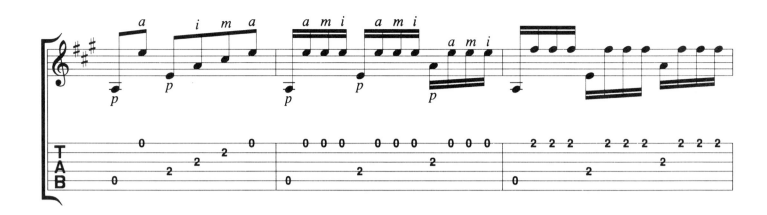

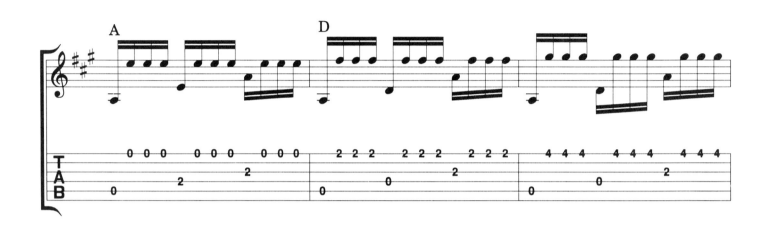

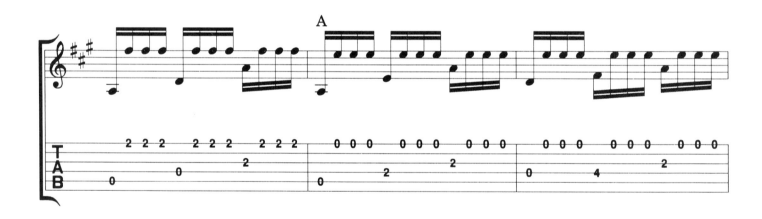

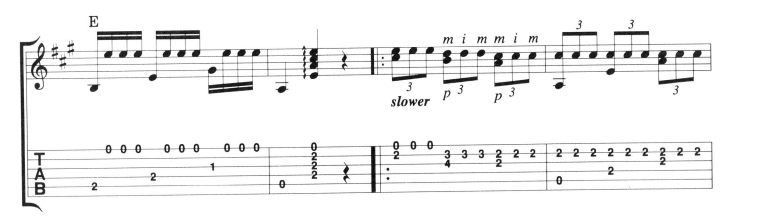

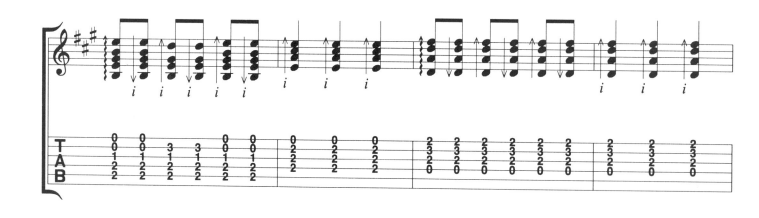

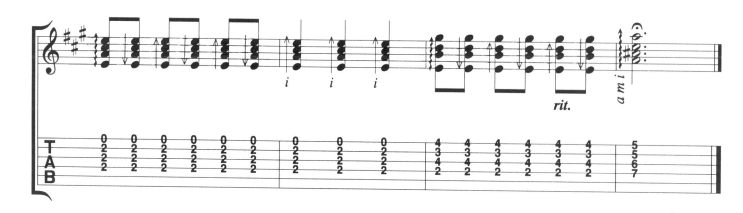

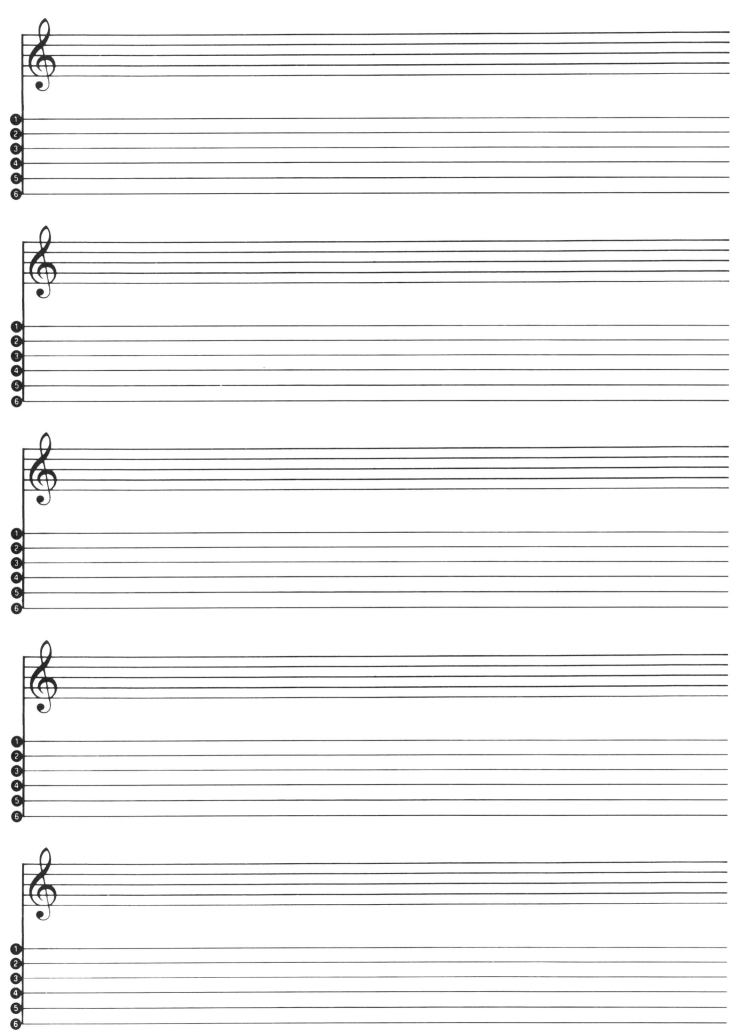

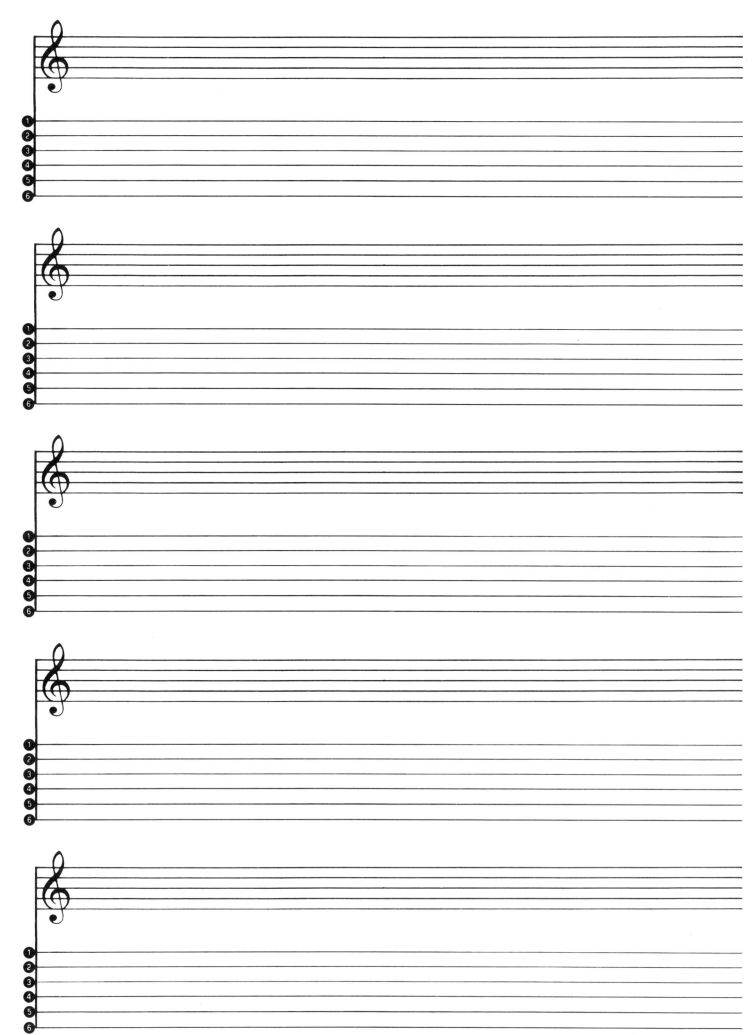